I0162508

Confessions of a Catholic Homeschool Mom by Karen Salstrom is an invitation to join her on her homeschooling journey. Her exploration of the basic questions—What is homeschooling? Is it worthwhile? How can I do it? Can I do it? Where does this fit into family life?—is delightful and insightful. Highly recommended.

Kimberly Hahn
Author of the Life-Nurturing Love series,
including *Legacy of Love: Biblical Wisdom for Parenting Teens and Young Adults*

Originally planning to homeschool to first grade, and now looking into the future, this book is a breath of fresh air! I'm not the only one to have doubts about my energy or ability to pick curriculum, or teach hard subjects that I struggled through, or afraid of wasting money on the wrong curriculum. Karen faces all these fears, and sets me free! I loved the writing style. Comparing each roadblock to Confession made it approachable and delightful. A quick but powerful read, it left me encouraged and empowered!

Jessica McAfee
FertilityCare practitioner, public speaker
and author, and wife of Shaun McAfee,
author and founder of EpicPew

Karen's book is a reminder that God can make masterpieces out of our messes. Sometimes we just have to be willing to trust and get messy. As one who is easily distracted, her discussion on vocation particularly hits home with me! The same Catholic life lessons she harkens to definitely apply to homeschooling. We fall down, ask forgiveness, do our penance, dust ourselves off, then get back up again and trust, trust, trust! You can do this!

One Mad Mom
Catholic blogger with Foeduscatholic.com

In this little book, Karen Salstrom helped me to see that I am not alone in my homeschooling misgivings. She writes with great wit and wonderful candor about many of the things you and I, Catholic homeschooling moms, experience in this fantastic and unpredictable journey. It is short, sweet, and edifying. If you need a good reminder that, *with the good Lord's grace*, you can succeed at this homeschool endeavor, read this book ASAP!

Valerie Staples
Homeschooling mom and wife of Tim Staples

I loved the confession analogy; most of us like "to-do" lists, but more of us are drawn to "What NOT TO DO!"—Good technique. The writing style is friendly and approachable, not too studious and not too fluffy. The examples are clear and not overly wordy. Karen revealed enough about her kids and still protected their deeper privacy.

Rose Sweet
Catholic author and speaker

CONFESSIONS

of a
Catholic Homeschool Mom

Karen L. Salstrom

LEONINE PUBLISHERS
PHOENIX, ARIZONA

Copyright © 2020 Karen L. Salstrom

All rights reserved. No part of this book may be reproduced or transmitted in any form or by any means, electronic or mechanical, including photocopying, recording, or by any information storage or retrieval system now existing or to be invented, without written permission from the respective copyright holder(s), except for the inclusion of brief quotations in a review.

Scripture texts in this work are taken from *The Holy Bible*, Revised Standard Version, Second Catholic Edition, copyright © 2006 by Ignatius Press, San Francisco.

Cover design by James Hrkach.

Published by

Leonine Publishers LLC
Phoenix, Arizona, USA

ISBN-13: 978-1-942190-59-2
Library of Congress Control Number: 2020908961
10 9 8 7 6 5 4 3 2 1

Visit us online at www.leoninepublishers.com
For more information: info@leoninepublishers.com

DEDICATION

To all my children and grandchildren, especially Elaine and Nick. It was through them that I learned the value of homeschooling, and how to truly follow God's direction to train up a child.

CONTENTS

INTRODUCTION

Confession is good for the soul. We Catholics know this through experience. In the eyes of Christians, we Catholics have the unique and wildly odd practice of systematically taking inventory of our blunders, trotting ourselves over to someone who can agree that we blew it, and then receiving our duly deserved punishment. Surely, that may be an outsider's view of the Sacrament of Reconciliation. However, Confession strengthens us in our journey, keeping us honest by giving us the chance to articulate where we've been and where we want to go. Ultimately, the Sacrament imparts grace for spiritual growth.

You might be wondering how exactly Confession, with its inherent form and structure, and homeschooling, with its loosely defined characteristics, make it into the same book. They seem too random to be able to fit neatly together. Most of the time, homeschooling isn't exactly a "neat and tidy" prospect. Books are everywhere. Papers, pencils, and other accoutrements lie strewn about. Kids sprawl in odd positions on floors and sofas (sometimes accompanied by a cuddling cat) or may sit surprisingly attentive at various tables throughout the house. You just never know how or where you'll find them. And housework, once a tedious and dreaded necessity, becomes a much-longed-for leisure activity, promising to whisk the weary homeschool mom away for a few moments of respite. For the most part, homeschooling does not resemble the comforting structure of the confessional, yet homeschooling, like participating in Confession, is a reflection of our lives.

Most of the daring adventurers, who throw themselves with reckless abandon into the abyss of homeschooling, do so for valid reasons. Everything from the desire for a faith component to a mistrust in a failing school system makes its way to the "Top 10 Reasons to Homeschool" list. From those with autism, to those with ADHD, to the typical child, to the genius IQ Stanford-bound students and their families have benefited from home education. We all come to homeschooling with the intention of "confessing" our mistrust in government education, which has fallen short, and praying for absolution and a new direction.

At times, along with good intentions and specific needs come pre-conceived notions of how to homeschool: super-structure, literature-based, Socratic method, un-schooling, car-schooling, curriculum-driven, child-driven. Every method known to man throughout the ages has made its way into potential home education methodology. Still, the question remains: What is the best way? We research. We investigate. We fret. We finally decide, only to fret over our decision. Finally, we settle…for a moment. Then suddenly, the unsuspecting homeschool mom collides with an Invisible Wall of Reality, often multiple times. She knew there was a wall, but convinced herself that her way was far superior to that of the world of formal education, which would somehow simply make the wall disappear.

This book is my confession as a mom who's traveled through that maze. It reveals how I managed to navigate some of those walls, at times being forced to reconstruct or even relocate them for the sake of a stronger home atmosphere. My account is given through the lens of a Catholic mother committed to taking seriously the training of her child. For those of you who have been at this for a while, perhaps some of these experiences will ring true and remind you that you are not the only one who, stumbling along, changed curriculum several times in one year. Or doubted your abilities. Or found yourself on the verge of quitting. And for those just starting out, maybe it will give you courage to face the day-to-day challenges in pursuit of the greatest reward a mother can receive: to enjoy the fruits of a job well done in raising and teaching her child, with the help of God.

Be forewarned. If you're looking for a "how-to" wrapped up in a nice, neat little spiritual package, it's not here. Rather than a training manual, this book is more of an account from someone who braved the muddy trenches and lived to tell the tale. Ultimately, this book is a therapeutic way (via that "confession" thing) of making sense of the strange, crazy, difficult at times, yet rewarding world of a Catholic mom who deliberately chose to swim upstream against the raging river of public education.

I am happy to be counted among your ranks, you who have heard and answered the calling—Catholic homeschooling moms.

CHAPTER 1:

BACKGROUND

Retreating from, Then Returning to Faith

As Maria in *The Sound of Music* so appropriately instructs in "Do-Re-Mi," all things have a beginning. To know the whole story, it helps to know the past. A glimpse into my history will set the stage for how I became a Catholic homeschooler.

In 1952, I was born into a wonderful Catholic family of Italian descent; however, we weren't solid, practicing Catholics. My brother and I were ushered into the Church via the obligatory Sacraments of Baptism, Reconciliation, First Holy Communion, and Confirmation, but regular weekly Mass was not on the radar. Somewhere in my memories are visions of my dad going with us to Mass at Easter and a few other scattered days. I remember wearing a frilly pink dress and an Easter bonnet secured to my head with an annoying piece of elastic. My brother, six years older than me, had the typical look of a preteen enduring the discomfort of a tie. I remember Dad in his dark suit and Mom in her sensibly modest 50s dress. However, since Dad was the only driver in the house, and being a proud American male of the Greatest Generation, who wasn't going to be told he had to go to church, our days as a family at Mass were limited.

I feel the need to sidebar on Dad's views on religion. Dad was raised Catholic in an Italian immigrant Catholic family, with a less-than-perfect male spiritual head of the household model. Even so, Dad was a believer; he simply wasn't well informed on how that ought to play out. As a child, he attended Saturday Catechism, just as I did later. He was under the tutelage of the elderly Sister Mary Calasanctious, as was I (believe it or not) years later. Perhaps because of his gender, or perhaps because of the era and the example of his own father, Dad set aside any need for formal involvement in religious disciplines.

Two incidents best portray his mindset, both of which attest to his aversion to others dictating to him. First, there was his ongoing "relationship" with the Jehovah's Witnesses door-to-door visitors. I remember multiple times these well-meaning (though misguided) souls would brave the neighborhood in search of converts. After several rounds with them, Dad finally came up with his solution. He devised a handwritten sign that said "NO JEHOVAHS," which he placed right at the doorway of the front porch. End of problem, though it was not in keeping with Catholic charity.

The second incident was even more pointed as it dealt not simply with Mother Church, but with our own parish. At the time of Vatican II, I was about twelve years old. I'm sure that the local parishes were clamoring to take advantage of these "new" innovations. All the changes seemed rather scandalous to the old-timers. The craziest request was that we pull those dusty Bibles from the shelves at home and begin reading them. Up to that point, all good Catholics had these visual reminders of the Faith in their homes but had no clue as to what to do with them. We relied on priestly readings and interpretations of Scripture at Mass.

Then on one bright Saturday morning, a nicely dressed couple from our parish appeared on our porch. Perhaps the Jehovah's sign gave them cause to pause, but they weren't Jehovah's Witnesses. So, "ding-dong," the bell was rung. What these poor, unsuspecting souls met was most certainly not what they were expecting. After all, they were Catholics from Saint John Vianney, and so were we, right? Wrong! We weren't *those* kinds of Catholics. When I answered the door, they introduced themselves, said who they were and where they were from. I passed the information to Dad, who blissfully reclined on the couch watching a San Francisco Giant's game. Dad retorted, "What do they want?" They answered that Father Cooke wanted everyone to start read their Bibles. My gaze returned to Dad, anticipating the explosion. I wasn't disappointed. In one of his louder voices, he let them know in no uncertain terms that they did not need to tell him what to do to be a Catholic. End of problem, though again it was not very charitable.

Even though Dad was not very forthcoming about his beliefs, the one comfort to my spirit is that I was able to have a short conversation with Dad before he died, during which I was assured of his faith.

How did these two experiences affect me as a Catholic, and later as a potential homeschooling mom? They obviously were not designed to keep me in the Church. Yet, both of these experiences gave me at least a foundation for standing up for my beliefs, even when faced with perceived "experts." Here, in a less-than-positive example, God helped me retrieve a nugget of gold for future use.

In contrast, my mother always displayed charity and love toward her neighbors. Her faith in God was a bit more visibly obvious. At times I would find her looking through her Bible or saying the Rosary. However, my strongest Catholic role model was my Italian paternal grandmother, Nana.

During the summers of my childhood, I spent most days with Nana. She and I would walk fourteen long city blocks in San Jose to St. Joseph Cathedral for Mass on Sunday, and at least one other day midweek for daily Mass. Every night after supper, Nana said her Rosary in the big, overstuffed chair in the front room. She was generous to neighbors and family, gentle and loving, and the picture of a Godly woman. Nana was one of the best Catholic models a young child could have. Unfortunately, she spoke very little English, and my Italian was pathetic. Other than the Blessed Mother, Nana is the one to whom I look even today for what a dedicated Catholic woman should be.

Childhood is never completely idyllic, and mine was no exception. On one sunny fourth- grade afternoon, in one of my more religious moods, I experienced what would become the beginning of a downward spiral away from the faith of my youth. My teacher was on yard duty, quizzing all the girls who circled around her like bees to honey, "What do you want to be when you grow up?" I listened intently to each girl's answer. Then it was my turn. I smiled happily and said, "I want to be a nun." An outburst of laughter (lead by my beloved teacher) pierced my ears. "Oh, Karen," she said through her chuckles, "you'll never be a nun!"

After that incident, I experienced a crisis of faith that followed me into my teen years. A post-Vatican II church in California unwittingly pulled at the loose thread caused by my teacher and began to unravel familiar spiritual foundations. Nearly overnight, Latin disappeared from the liturgy and veils became passé. The priest inexplicably faced the faithful during Mass, instead of the *ad orientem* to which we were accustomed. Birth control was supported by some priests and nuns, and nuns in some orders eliminated the habits I had come to love.

Yet the one thing that caused the most impact happened in my fourteenth year: Nana, my Spiritual Compass, passed away. Her absence at a critical time in my formation and the lack of her example and unconditional love, coupled with a weak Catholic identity at home, and a changing church, made for the perfect storm.

A flurry of hormones added to the mix, then I was off to the races in a series of less than optimal personal choices. The worst of these ended in a marriage to a non-Catholic, two children, and an early divorce. That is not to say that God did not work good out of the mess I had created. What should have been one of the worst times in my life actually became one of the best.

First, there was the blatant contrast to the Nana Ideal. I observed over time the emptiness of a life without faith, and that knowledge would eventually help to catapult me forward again. And second, I was blessed with two beautiful boys (incidentally, both were instrumental in my return to faith and Mother Church), who continue to be a joy in my life. Still, the road would take me on a sidetrack through Protestantism for over thirty years before coming home to Catholicism for good.

God is amazing, but I suppose you know that. His omniscience and omnipresence are not always clear until you've been through some of life's challenges, and it was never more evident to me than in the circumstances of my return to the Catholic Church. When my boys were in elementary school, the oldest asked if he could go to Sunday school. What a crazy request! What second-grade boy in his right mind, after five days of drudgery in public education, would choose to torture himself on a Sunday morning as well? Being an over-achieving single mom, I entertained the idea of the Catholic Church...for about a minute. What made the Catholic Church an unlikely choice was some poor advice I received in the early 1970s: a well-meaning (though completely uninformed) friend said that I would not be welcome at the Catholic Church after my divorce, and definitely could not receive Communion. I willingly accepted this false fact from the poorly catechized blind leading me, the even less catechized blind. Naturally, it seemed crazy to send my children to a church where I was not welcome. Consequently, I quickly sought out a Protestant alternative.

We eventually settled on a Reformed church. I will forever be grateful for those years because it forced me to actually read a Bible, and my faith and love for Christ was rekindled. Then in 1989, I met a dear man at a singles group. Soon after, we committed to each other and married, blending our families and five children. A few years later, after a failed ability to conceive, we adopted a child from Uzbekistan. Finally in 1997, we joyfully accepted guardianship of our first grandson, who became much more like a son as we raised him.

At some point along the way, a growing sense of discontentment with Protestantism haunted me and Roger, my husband. Consequently, we fell into what is commonly known as "church hopping." The experience was always the same. We would begin at a particular denomination, fully intending it would be permanent, yet, somewhere along the way, there was some type of teaching that didn't quite seem right or someone would mistreat our young grandson, and off we'd go in search again for the right church. We like to call it our Wandering in the Desert years. Little did we know that even through those days of discontent, God was pointing us toward the Promised Land of objective Truth in His Church.

Throughout this process, we had many faith discussions with one of my boys and his wife. This younger son had met and married a Catholic woman and converted. Slowly over time, and in the most relational way, they planted seeds on the differences between Protestantism and Catholicism. One of the ongoing themes was authority. We had never thought about the need for an authoritative final word on matters of faith, particularly in regard to Holy Scripture. We began to understand why all the churches we attended had contrasting views on important issues: they each thought they were the final authority.

Those conversations with this son and his wife, along with a loaner book of Scott Hahn's *Rome Sweet Home*, culminated in a huge, "Aha!" moment for me. Roger followed closely behind, although his was a much more analytical, investigative approach. So, after more than thirty years away, I became a revert. Yes, a re-version of myself, better and renewed. Roger became a convert after being a lifelong (up to that point) Protestant. Thankfully, the grandchild for whom we were guardians was confirmed at age fourteen and continues in his Catholic Faith.

Throughout my journey, first back to faith and then back to Catholicism, I became increasingly aware of the awesome responsibility parents have in their children's education. "Train up a child in the way he should go, and when he is old he will not depart from it" (Proverbs 22:6). There it is, one of those pesky little mandates from God that leaves you little wiggle room. But what does it mean?

There are many ways we train our children. We start out early with walking and talking, and move rapidly toward the dreaded behind-the-wheel training in the family car. We treasure each milestone as a personal success. Interspersed through it all are moments for us to instill ethics, morals, and faith. Then, for some odd reason, when our precious ones reach kindergarten age, we turn them over for several hours a day to, basically, a stranger—one whose worldview will impact and influence the child God entrusted to us.

Training a child is so much more than first steps and moving from "ga-ga" to coherent speech. The most important training for our children is what we invest in developing their character. Even if little Johnny never gets to Harvard, if he learns the more important lesson of developing a moral compass by knowing, loving, and serving God, he will be miles ahead in the education that counts.

My journey into homeschooling was similar to my journey back to Rome: slow, with revelations along the way. Remember, we have our own unique version of "Yours, Mine, and Ours," and we had a few epiphany moments. With seven, there's plenty of time to get it right, right? Since our children span over twenty-seven years, we experienced school in several arenas. One was in the public-school arena, another was in private schools, and the final was our admission that homeschooling was where God wanted our family. All along there were hurdles that brought our family closer to the Homeschooling Finish Line, little blips that caused us to pause. One certainty is that the closer we came to homeschooling in earnest, the deeper we came to realize that to fully embrace the commission of training up a child, education decisions need to be thoughtful and deliberate. For me and for our family, homeschooling was the eventual and only answer.

CHAPTER 2:

SELF-EXAMINATION

The First Part of a Good Confession

Any good confession begins with an honest self-examination. So here goes...

When the oldest boys were born in the early 1970s, homeschooling never crossed my mind. If it had, I would have equated it with some kind of Hippie-Drop-Out-of-Society Movement taking place on some wilderness compound under the radar of the U.S. Government School Authorities. Besides, as a single mom it would have been virtually impossible to do school at home. Surviving on one income is difficult enough, but having no income would have been a recipe for disaster. Instead, my two boys attended public schools. And why not? If public school was good enough for me, it should be good enough for my boys, and at that point, public school was what nearly everyone was doing.

Although there were some issues during those years, both of the boys had high IQs, and for a time they were part of a special program. However, that ended in elementary school. Subsequent middle and high schools did little to challenge their capabilities and even less to motivate them. Not a surprise. Public schools are notorious for teaching down to the lowest common denominator, which is great if you're in the middle, but not so good if you are on either end of the educational spectrum. You'll either be lost or, in my boys' cases, bored to tears.

So, there were wrinkles. But being a young, single working mom, I was oblivious to most of these pitfalls. Like most parents, I thought we were supposed to let the education experts do what they did best: educate.

One other factor that clouded this early time frame was that I had wandered from faith. I had no idea there was an actual mandate from God that I should be training my children, or that such a mandate applied to their education. The only lessons I found necessary were those that affected mundane, daily life: eat your broccoli, don't put your shirt on backwards, clear a path on the floor to your bed, don't punch your brother in the nose, be careful crossing the street, and don't shove your brother into the street. I couldn't think beyond those basics, so public school it was.

The next three children (my step-children) were also public school educated. Being part of a blended family, I came into their lives when they had already been in school for several years. Again, homeschooling was not a typical option in our area, so it was not even an afterthought for us. The few families homeschooling were not the off-the-radar types, and stood as exceptions to the rule. Looking back, even if we had seriously entertained the possibility, logistically, homeschooling was not a realistic option in a shared-custody world.

In all fairness, a public education for these first five children offered some positives. All of them were involved in an abundance of activities, from sports to theater, and landed great careers as adults.

The next of the seven children was the daughter we adopted from Uzbekistan. Right from the start, we needed to develop some kind of plan to bridge the language barrier, if nothing else. We were familiar with immersion education and thought it would be a perfect setting for our new daughter. However, when we adopted her, we were unaware of her treatment at the hands of an abusive family, followed by further abuse in an orphanage in Uzbekistan. Consequently, we were taken by surprise when she displayed negative behavior. She eventually was diagnosed with post-traumatic stress disorder, as well as reactive attachment disorder. For a few years, we placed her in a private school, but for middle school, her therapist challenged us with a concept that would be best for her: homeschooling.

Homeschooling?

That was our first introduction to this odd method of education. I suddenly felt as if we were destined to be thrust into some backwoods life, living in constant suspicion of "The Gov'ment." By then, we had read many more current reports regarding how well government schools fare in exit studies. Consequently, we thought maybe that wasn't such a bad idea. However, handling her education ourselves made no sense. We needed some way to handle a child who balked at our authority due to her condition, yet this professional counselor wanted me to keep her home—all day, every day—and become not only her parent-authority-figure, but her education-authority-figure as well. The nerve!

After a bit of resistance (well, yeah!), and under the advice of the counselor, we took on this foreign task.

Our daughter completed middle school and three years of high school at home. We hit some blips in the process, but we fared much better than when she was in public school.

By her senior year, we began to gravitate back to the familiar. In our defense, this was all with good (or so we thought) reason: we felt she needed a transition so that she would be more prepared for possible college coursework. Feeling confident (ha!) in that decision, we enrolled her in a small Christian school. Not the best plan. Her attachment disorder symptoms increased, causing extreme difficulties at home and school; she did not complete her senior year. Instead, she worked hard and obtained a GED a few years later.

All things considered and in retrospect, finishing out high school in the homeschool setting would have likely been the better choice for her, but we were still in the transition stage of embracing home-schooling as the best option for education.

The final phase in our homeschooling journey was with the grandson we raised. He was born with auditory processing disorder (a neurologically based hearing issue), which caused some speech and milestone delays. The funny thing about so-called delays is that in the greater scheme of things, each child progresses at the rate he/she was intended to progress. Does the average, the norm, matter at all? Children seem to advance at their own rate and God's timing.

Nevertheless, certain issues needed addressing. Auditory processing can prevent a child from differentiating between sounds. Our son couldn't distinguish consonants. For example, he may interpret the spoken word "maybe" to be "baby." Many times, entire meanings are lost in the wake of an auditory processing issue. Fortunately, although it is an issue, it is not insurmountable.

In order to get our boy ready for first grade, we worked extensively at home on phonics and visual cues to speech by having him watch our lips as we spoke. We also trained him to listen in context so that the word he could not decipher would make more sense. Finally (here we go again), we believed he was ready for first grade and enrolled him in a small, private Christian school. Things went marginally well, but he was having such difficulty in hearing with background noise in the class that, under the advice of a physician, we switched gears to homeschool in the second grade. This time, we were a bit more prepared.

We perceived this time around as being our all-in-to-the-end experience. Was it a challenge? Yes. Was I stretched as a mom? Yes. Did I feel inadequate at times? Yes. But was it worth it? YES! Our grandson graduated from high school in 2015 with nearly a 4.0, primarily because I would not accept any work below a B. He was accepted into several private and public universities, and is on the road to a degree in philosophy, with a communications minor. All those revisions I required of him seem to have paid off.

As shocking as it sounds, not all students fit into the typical constraints offered by government schools. Okay, you already know that. In our case, schools were poorly equipped to deal with our children, some of whom were atypical and did not fit into the public education box. With circumstances ranging from high IQs not being challenged, to specific psychological needs, to physiological challenges, homeschooling offered a greater opportunity for success. It is often the case that government education fails children in many ways due to the one-size-fits-all mentality.

Thankfully, our children lead good lives, both personally and professionally, but the negative effects of being exposed to government schools leaves us free to say that they excelled in spite of what was lacking in their public school educations. What they have accomplished is more of a testimony to their own abilities, intellects, and personalities, rather than being a compliment to a stellar school experience.

We do have some regrets. When I glance back at the educational paths we walked with them, I can see areas where each would have benefited from home education. I know now what I wish I had known then. Because education can be tailored to each child's weaknesses, strengths, and learning style, homeschooling is an ideal choice for most children.

This book is not meant to be a thorough assessment of public government schools. Instead, I am presenting an admission of my experiences and failures in home education—my sins. As the account here unfolds, know that this story is centered on homeschooling our last in line, one we homeschooled virtually from start to finish. He was the only one of our children who was afforded that experience. Because we came so late to the homeschooling party, our home education story, both the good and bad, is reflected through him.

CHAPTER 3:

FIRST CONFESSION

The Sin of Succumbing to Temptation

*"I'm going to use (x, y, z) curriculum.
Everyone says it is great, and public schools
even use it. Why bother to reinvent the wheel?"*
~ Spoken by homeschool moms everywhere

Indeed!

"Lead us not into temptation." That line from
The Lord's Prayer was written for homeschoolers! I found myself being tempted in several areas:
1) to mimic the public school model, 2) to envy
other homeschoolers, and 3) to seek validation by
over-scheduling. Each of these avenues brought
their own set of complications.

If This Is School, It Had Better Look Like School!

Before I began homeschooling, I thought that
every homeschooling mom immediately selected
the best curriculum, executed her school days with
ease, and cranked out cheerful, successful little

homeschoolers who looked forward to each day with Teacher Mom. This fantasy couldn't have been further from reality.

I went into this venture with a healthy degree of fear. I expected I would never get through this intimidating task. Of course, looking at it as a task was likely not my best foot forward, but part of that fear was warranted. As I merged onto the treacherous road to Homeschool Land, I suddenly came to a most frightening realization: "I have no clue what I'm doing!"

What in the world had I gotten myself into? Intellectually, I knew it was where our family needed to be, but I was completely unprepared. Not only did I not know how to homeschool, I had no inkling as to *what* I did not know. Confused and overwhelmed, I frantically began to research. Most of what I saw was akin to being plucked out of the Good Old USA and being dropped into the middle of an obscure foreign village, knowing that my survival depended upon communicating in the new language, yet never even hearing that tongue until right at that moment.

Hyperventilation ensued. Fear gripped my otherwise rational mind. So, I did what any reasonably panicked new home-educator might do: I fearfully fled to the familiar. What that meant for me was to design my day and my curriculum to look exactly like public school. I went to the local teacher supply store for supplies. What I thought would be a no-brainer trip became another source of fear and indecision. But I was on a mission! Here was what I did in my flurry:

I bought one of those individual wooden desks with the cubby under the seat.
RESULT: My son hated it. In fact, he sat in it once, possibly.

I divided the day systematically into 50-minute segments.
RESULT: That was a joke! I could never keep within those time frames.

I set up an unrealistic number of courses to match traditional schools.
RESULT: We both became frustrated and disappointed.

I got some of the same curriculum available in public schools.
RESULT: Oy vey!

By gravitating to the familiarity of the public school model, I unwittingly set up the seeds of failure, thus reinforcing my belief that I would fail. Talk about a revolving door! Why in the world did I think that what did not work while he was in public school would somehow miraculously be perfectly suited for homeschool?

So, why did we pull him out of public school?

It was time to regroup.

Envy, Thy Name Is Woman (with apologies to Shakespeare)

Once we took the plunge into private home-schooling, the methodology, curriculum, and approach doors flew wide open. That was the good news/bad news. I found myself in conversations with seasoned homeschool moms, each of whom knew with absolute certainty her methods were correct. Each support group became a place for me to wallow in the development of a new issue: HSLS (Homeschooler Self-Esteem Loss Syndrome). While these well-meaning ladies shared their perfectly planned days, successfully schooling four or five children, I sat in wonder, contemplating my failures with only one child at home.

More Is Better, Right?

What baffled me even more than their supposed teaching expertise was the quantity of interesting extra-curricular activities they effortlessly (so I thought) managed to fit into their schedules: acting, piano, voice lessons, gymnastics, horseback riding, art, outer space exploration. (Okay, blatant hyperbole on that last one, but you get the picture.) The point is that it seemed as though I was supposed to work all kinds of "experiences" for my child into my bursting-at-the-seams schedule. After all, we were Homeschool Moms! Opportunities were limited only by our imaginations, and perhaps our wallets.

I must say, I fell into the busyness model for a while. We would rush through regular schoolwork so that we could then rush off to the activity, co-op class, or field trip of the day. And on those days when our son balked for having to (yet again) leave the house for some activity, my job entailed being the cheerleading advocate for said escapade.

Don't get me wrong. There were some activities that proved very beneficial in his growth. One of the best things he did was musical theatre, which helped him develop the confidence and ability to speak in public settings. Eventually, however, as I dragged him metaphorically kicking and screaming from the house, the perceived benefits of my newly adopted overscheduled life began to fade in the shadow of the developing need for some calm and peace.

Coming to Terms with the Inevitable: Pick Something!

Re-evaluation. Regrouping. Revision.

I was slowly discovering that the Homeschool Road was not necessarily a straight and narrow, one-way path. There were side streets, U-turns, caution lights, and even a few stop signs to observe in order to make it the best road trip for all passengers. At this point, re-evaluation was critical.

First, I needed to remember that homeschooling was the right decision. Second, I forced myself to examine why I'd fallen into this never-ending roller coaster with our curriculum schizophrenia and hyperactive activities frenzy. The time of discovery helped me fine-tune the homeschool journey for our family and our child.

All of this is to point out that sometimes the wheel *needs* reinventing! The key, I was discovering, is to watch and listen to your child. One size does not fit all. Government schools fail miserably in this fact. Learning your child's strengths and weaknesses is the first imperative in discerning how best to educate him. Although I was a slow learner, the seeds for this necessity were planted early on in the journey.

Ongoing awareness is essential in order to avoid succumbing to the sin of temptation.

CHAPTER 4:

SECOND CONFESSION

The Sin of Doubt

"Modest doubt is called the beacon of the wise."
~ William Shakespeare

Who among us, while traversing the rough terrain of life, would not welcome a beacon to light the path? So many decisions would be so much easier if each came with a laser beam pointing to the correct direction. According to William Shakespeare, there is such brilliance in a most unexpected form: doubt. When researching the word "doubt," we find that it is a feeling of uncertainty or lack of conviction, which is not a very inspiring beacon. Consequently, this begs the question: What could Shakespeare have possibly meant?

In its purest form, doubt is a form of questioning. In the scientific method, we see it in the formation of theories. Throughout the steps of scientific methodology, there remains an uncertainty (doubt) that accompanies the theorist until he reaches the end of his quest. First, in his curiosity about the world, he observes something that causes him to doubt that things are exactly as they seem. Next, he uses that doubt as a springboard to form a question. He then constructs a hypothesis to fine-tune his question, and the fun begins. In his quest to discover whether his initial observations warranted the hypothesis, he embarks upon a journey involving experiments. At the end of his research, he either discovers that his experiments proved the doubts were valid, or he is drawn to a conclusion that shows all his data is in support of the original hypothesis. But he is not finished. He must then replicate the process in order to prove it was not simply by random chance that he was able to allay all doubt and come to his conclusion.

When done properly, experiments should carry an element of doubt; if doubt did not accompany the process, one might be tempted to jump to a premature and incorrect conclusion. In fact, without a degree of doubt, a person might subconsciously, or perhaps even more overtly, manipulate data in order to justify his conclusion, thus creating a self-fulfilling prophecy. In this way, doubt provides the open mind needed for accurate scientific discovery, and reflects Shakespeare's thoughts in the quote above.

But why does doubt get such a bad reputation?

One reason may be the story of Saint Thomas the Apostle. His story in the Gospel of John reflects his desire for physical proof in order for him to believe in Christ's Resurrection. Ah, the scientific need for proof. Christ's subsequent response—*Blessed are those who have not seen and believed*—may have in part been responsible for the nickname with which we are all familiar: Doubting Thomas. That tag is used in a variety of contexts and is considered less than flattering. However, Jesus's response might actually attest to the two forms of belief: visual belief, as when the apostles ran to the tomb to see evidence of Jesus's Resurrection, and internal belief without visual proof. Though it is unclear whether the words Jesus spoke in response were meant as a rebuke, Thomas clearly did not doubt belief in Jesus himself. His response, "My Lord and my God," is evidence of that. In fact, he along with the other apostles went on to a fruitful ministry of bringing Christ to the world. Even so, the negative title from this one isolated incident remains. Sorry, Saint Thomas.

But there is a form of doubt that is destructive if allowed to go unchecked. That type of doubt was clearly in play as I embarked upon the homeschool journey. There were three distinct areas where my new nemesis, Doubt, tried to sabotage my efforts: doubting the decision, internalizing doubts from friends and family, and allowing myself to become the pawn of doubt.

Doubting the Decision

When I began homeschooling our youngest, it was under personal protest, at least internally. We were rounding the home stretch in the parenting race, and I was smelling the hay in the barn, running on able haunches, trotting off in the final leg of the race. Understand, this was the last child in line and we were not prepared to re-route our parenting paradigm.

When we initially enrolled our youngest in a small private school, we began the year with great hope. It seemed that maybe this round of private schooling might work for our family, until two defining incidents offered reality checks.

The first was less of an incident and more of an observance. Apparently, our son's grades were not up to par, which was a huge shock to us, given that we knew he was extremely bright. Unfortunately, his grades were not reflecting that fact. His teacher placed the blame on his being "social" (buzz word for talkative). We suggested he be seated toward the front of the class. With that solution in place, we anticipated he would settle in and grades would improve. Looking back and considering his auditory issue, the social nature he exhibited was more likely due to being distracted, which then caused him to turn his attention to other students rather than the teacher. Unfortunately, his performance in this setting never rose to the level to which we knew he was capable. Even so, we were willing to accept this minor problem so that he might benefit from the traditionally coveted socialization that is provided in a formal school setting, a bubble of illusion that soon burst.

The second incident was the one that helped us make our decision for homeschooling. We were a little over two-thirds through the school year when we received a concerned call from the school. We were told that our son—our sweet, kind-hearted, gentle son—had put his hands around another boy's neck, and the other child's parent was registering a formal complaint. Our first-grade son having a formal complaint of violence on his school record was impossible to comprehend. He was the kind of kid who compassionately went to the aid of an injured child at a shopping mall play area. Were we to believe that he had suddenly gone from being gentle to being a violent monster bent on strangling an innocent playmate?

A disciplinary meeting was scheduled. What transpired is a blur, but the outcome was a half-day onsite suspension, which took place on a day of fun for the rest of the students: pajama day. His punishment was that he was seated by himself in an adjacent room—in his pajamas—for several hours while his classmates enjoyed games and snacks. He could hear the fun, but was barred from participating.

Long story short, it took three weeks (long after his school discipline) to discover that the boys in question were doing something they did often: playing Power Rangers. All three boys were doing head locks, but ours was the only one disciplined. A person might wonder why it took our son three weeks to debrief the incident, but this was common for him since auditory processing caused a delay in language. The processing portion of processing delays can play out not only in difficulty differentiating sounds, but also in sorting out events in order to give an account of situations. Fortunately, as his language developed, this little problem was resolved. However, because he was unable to articulate the sequence of events at the school meeting, he was assumed to be the sole perpetrator. Seeing that his auditory issues could create this type of scenario, we decided to follow a physician's suggestion to homeschool him.

You would think making a decision that was best for our child would eliminate all doubt. You would be oh, so wrong.

Doubt took time to settle in, pushed down for a time by a frenzy of research into curriculum (a nightmare in its own rite), then online and in-store purchasing of materials. Once the dust settled, Doubt found a sweet little home in my heart. A big part of that was due to a certain level of expectations, most of which were unrealistic. I was in the middle of an evening degree-completion program at a local college, with its inherent massive amounts of homework, but I created this dream-like expectation that he and I would work side by side, doing our respective schoolwork. Mom and son. Enduring the suffering and successes. In it together. What could possibly go wrong?

The unrealistic expectation to maintain a heavy, personal school schedule coupled with an unexpected anxiety that accompanied my new role as teacher set up the elements for a perfect Doubt Storm to brew. By the third day of trying to maintain the schedule of teach-study-teach, Doubt choked out any shred of optimistic hope. The dark cloud of Doubt overshadowed all my efforts. I struggled to develop lesson plans, and then once they were established, I struggled to follow them. My college homework piled up. The one recurring question that simultaneously gave me both objectivity and abject fear was, "WHAT WAS I THINKING?"

The great thing about fear is that it can cause you to realize that something needs to happen. In the wild, if a person is confronted by a bear, there are choices. Faint, run, or stand very tall, stretch upward and yell. I'm told the latter is quite effective, though I've not tested it. Similarly, in my situation I needed to decide how to proceed. If I did not do so—and quickly—not one, but two students would be frustrated and fail. This is where I had to take a serious look at the situation. My choices were 1) to continue in the same direction, which obviously wasn't working, 2) to give up and try again in public or private school so that I could finish my degree, or 3) discontinue the degree program and devote my complete attention to our son's schooling. It didn't take very long to decide. It became clear that our son's need for a homeschool setting with a focused mom was more pressing than my desire to finish my degree. Once I settled that issue, the doubt I had in the decision to homeschool began to fade.

One doubt down.

Friends (and Family) Are Friends Forever, Unless You Homeschool

"Why would you take him out of school?"
"Is that even legal?"
"But you don't have a teaching credential."
"What about socialization?"
"You can't get them graduated and ready for college this way."

Ah, the voices of those with only your best interest in mind. Having homeschooled our daughter for a short time through high school, I was not prepared for opposition. Yet there it was. As I heard and deflected each objection from family and friends, my confidence took a new hit. Doubt didn't waste any time taking advantage of each of their concerns. It was not as if I had not thought about each complaint and hurdle in homeschooling. In fact, that was all part of the initial decision process.

Of course, I researched the legality in our state; that was not going to be an issue. In our state, there were actually no laws governing homeschooling. Compared to those states that set up a myriad of hoops through which to leap, California was a breeze. The only real requirement was to file a Private School Affidavit which gave the details of address, number of students, etc. There was no list of approved curriculum or courses of study. Consequently, a teaching credential was not required. Even so, the State Department of Education website proved useful to see what subjects were studied, and we used that resource extensively.

Despite of the lack of regulation, one concern arose because California was notorious for sending truancy officers to the home of "absent" students. We heard horror stories of children removed from their homes temporarily by overzealous social workers. However, there was a degree of peace of mind offered if we joined the Home School Legal Defense Association (HSLDA), a non-profit group of pro-bono lawyers who represent homeschoolers should such an incident arise. In doing so, we knew our rights would be protected from illegal actions against our private school.

In public school, socialization is overrated at its best and dangerous at its worst. Anyone who has observed how children in public school interact with each other, as well as with adults, understands the lack of finesse and ability these children have in basic social skills, and the abundance of bullying that rules the schoolyard. Children play out a miniature version of *Lord of the Flies* on the playground, leaving the weaker, more awkward kids in the dust of the School Social Ladder, which is where the self-esteem issues are perpetuated. When the emotional bullying cycle goes unchecked, it can escalate to being physical, with most kids unwilling or afraid to involve adults in their perpetual suffering.

In contrast, private homeschooling offers a unique methodology for a more natural, multi-generational type of socialization. True, school is at home and interaction there is limited to the student's siblings and parents. However, that is not the complete story. There are numerous and varied possibilities for outside interactions: co-ops, support groups, classes in the arts, field trips, and playdates. The list is endless, although needs discernment so overscheduling does not become the norm. Within these additional opportunities, both students and their parents are present, creating a safety net to "catch" a child who might fall into unacceptable behavior. How does that play out? Since most homeschool families have left the school system at least in part to develop character within their children, there are higher expectations. In group settings such as field trips, parents are present. They are available and engaged in watching and correcting any imminent issues. Students are seldom left on their own in a recess setting, so there is no backdrop for the type of bullying seen on playgrounds. From the earliest age, a student learns to interact both with students of varying ages, as well as adults. In fact, it is not uncommon to hear from outsiders that they are impressed with how one of these students speaks with ease when conversing with adults.

Since I'd done my homework and was satisfied with the benefits, why did the inquisition from friends and family rattle me? Looking back, I can identify a few reasons.

First, even though I knew other people had been successful, I was a newbie. I'd not even begun! Because it was all speculative at this point, it was hard to argue that I would be capable and that my child would reap all these promised benefits.

Second, and more of a hurdle, is that I came from a circle of family and friends steeped in public education. In fact, many of them were public school teachers. In essence, I was being challenged by seasoned experts who seemingly knew the field inside and out. They had degreed credentials. How could I not feel intimidated? I had absolutely no expertise, no experience, and no successes, or so I thought. In actuality, my experience as a parent in educating my children was filled with successes: crawling, walking, talking, potty training, autonomy versus obedience, faith in God, and so forth. I realized I needed to revise how I thought about what I had already done in educating my child.

In retrospect, I can see how my choice to homeschool may have seemed a rejection of my friends and family's *de facto* choice in education, a minimization of their education degrees. If parents could teach children at home, does that mean a degree in teaching is worthless? I will be the first to say that is not so. There are wonderful teachers in the public setting. It isn't the teachers for whom I have little respect; it is the system. Whatever the reason for the instant opposition from these people in my life, it became a place for Doubt to visit me in full force.

The outcome of my final decision to homeschool resulted in loss of respect from some friends and family. Although their reactions were disappointing, I knew that making an unpopular (though correct) stand often reaps such an end result.

Unfortunately, there was an even greater Doubt hovering over me.

We've Identified the Enemy, and It Is...ME!

"Honey, don't be so hard on yourself."
~ Spoken by every mother
to her child at some time

These words of encouragement, often accompanied by a hug, are often repeated by parents to children. Unfortunately, Mom's comforting words don't always follow us into adult life. How many times do we feel inadequate, in spite of our best efforts? How often do we carry with us that invisible baseball bat because we just *know* we are going to blow it and will need that bat nearby in order to beat ourselves up?

These feelings of failure aren't new nor unique. They simply reflect the ongoing human condition of trying to control our surroundings, situations, and our lives. As we move through childhood on our way to the Holy Grail of adulthood, our self-esteem takes many hits, oft times at the mercy of kids in our schools and on our playgrounds. Boys tease the girls with hurtful name-calling, and develop a complex pecking order among the other boys. Girls aren't any better. With their affinity for cliques and fashion, they pass judgements that determine each other's social standing, often tied to whether attire or hairstyles meet the clique's approval.

As these strikes against childhood egos play out, we watch the seemingly well-adjusted and confident ones succeed at everything, and then measure ourselves against their successes. Little did we know, the ones we envied were enviously watching the ones they envied. Unfortunately, these rituals of acceptance or inclusion define us within the social structure from a very young age.

We become so good at beating ourselves up that by the time we are adults, we have subconsciously (though inaccurately) accepted that we are inferior and less than adequate. This identity crisis haunts many well into their adult lives, often creating roadblocks to excellence in relationships.

The effects of childhood self-esteem issues played into my own lack of confidence to homeschool successfully, and I became my own worst enemy through these doubts.

Remember our friend Willie Shakespeare? He seemed to believe that doubt could be a positive thing. *Modest doubt is called the beacon of the wise.* How in the world could I or, for that fact, any new homeschooler glean something positive in light of the doubts being thrust upon us from within and without? I can't answer for everyone; I can only relate how I finally dealt with it.

First, it was important for me to revisit our reasons for homeschooling, because that was our foundation, the homeschool rock that we laid in order to build this new educational fortress. Those reasons had not changed for us:

1. Our son had a need for a less intrusive auditory environment. We needed to deal with that in order to train him for his future and get him ready for higher education.
2. The school system is fraught with an inherent structure that teaches to the middle; we knew that our son, despite the auditory issue, was well above that middle in intellect and needed nurturing in order to develop to his fullest.
3. Public schools had become a breeding place for political ideology (indoctrinations in environmental studies, promotion of abortion, support for alternative lifestyles and "marriages," etc.), which was not compatible with our Christian values, and even more so when we became Catholic.
4. Time allotted for the three Rs, has diminished, sharing classroom time with these social issues, meaning less real education taking place.
5. The style of socialization did not promote multi-generational, ethical, or positive interactions. We wanted more for our son

than for him to merely become like the boys on the playground.

Once I regained my bearings, the voice of Doubt was quieted.

Second, I needed to remind myself once again of God's Word with regard to parenting: "Train up a child in the way he should go, and when he is old he will not depart from it" (Proverbs 22:6). I began to wonder: How can a parent completely train a child who is constantly being subjected to a worldview in contrast to faith, which is what parents are up against in public education, and sadly sometimes even in private education. Here is how it works.

You love your child and diligently instill what you know to be true about God as he grows in his early years. Then suddenly when he is five or six, you relinquish that job for six hours a day to a stranger. At best, the teacher might be a Christian, but if it is a public school, the teacher will not be allowed to reference God with regards to any curriculum. In fact, the teacher is under pressure to keep God outside the perimeter of the school. Also, curriculum can be generally lacking, and in many cases is not accurate about historic events that are tied to faith, such as the Crusades and the Spanish Inquisition. In some states such as ours, positive references to religion often refers to Islam, where Jihad has been portrayed in a positive light as part of the new goal of Social Studies, as opposed to pure history. Because social studies can easily become subjective based

43

upon the agenda and desired outcome of educators, the term "social studies" should always be a cause of concern.

Science is no better. God's role in creation is ignored. Issues pertaining to life and sex are taught from a viewpoint decidedly lacking in, if not hostile to, Christian thought, even as early as kindergarten. Even worse, teachers may harbor anti-religious sentiments that permeate and influence his/her methodology and logic. One way or another, your child will take away something you won't like. This pattern sets the stage for many of our children leaving their faith.

Perhaps you think private schools may be a better option, but they are expensive and may not be the panacea you seek. Remain wary of teachers. Unfortunately, your child may not have one, but rather several throughout the day. Do you absolutely know they will support your Catholic worldview? Even in Catholic schools there are either Protestant or progressive Catholic teachers who balk at some Magisterial teachings.

Friendships are another concern in both private and public settings. Your student will be making friends over which you have no control. At times in private schools there even are children of atheists whose parents choose a school for its education value, not faith component. These may be the new friends in your child's life, bringing into the friendship the worldview of their parents.

Beyond the faith element, some habitually truant or troublesome children find their way into private schools as their parents struggle to find ways to rein them in. Keep in mind that many children are attracted to fun, outspoken classmates. Some problem students fit those personality traits and may become friends with your child.

Perhaps these issues don't concern you. After all, the world is complex and these children represent the tapestry of life they will eventually encounter. Others may argue that your children may have a positive effect on these other children. Both of these may contain a degree of truth, but our family did not feel childhood was the time for such experimentation. Good and bad both exist in the world and we should all try to influence others with our faith, but early childhood may not be the right time for such a task, especially when the school authorities are not likely to side with the Christian view. Homeschooling, on the other hand, not only provides a great degree of control over the curriculum, but also all social interactions, which in turn affords a greater ability to protect, guard, and shape a child's developing faith and ethics.

All these factors helped quiet doubts in me.

Finally, I needed to remember that my friends and family members are not privy to the actual needs of my child. They may be experts in their fields or in how they decide to raise and educate their own children, but none of them had my child's best interest in mind, no matter how much they said they did. Only a parent can lay claim to that honor, as bestowed upon each parent by God Himself. We are caretakers for the souls He allows us to borrow during this pilgrimage, and charges us with guiding them in making what we feel are the very best decisions. We are responsible only to Him and must answer our calling. Once this became clear, I was able to finally let the voices fade into the distance.

Did Doubt completely go away? Goodness, no! But I came much closer to the concept of our friend, Mr. Shakespeare. I was able to let the *modest* doubts in, so that they would illuminate my possible choices each step of the way. If big, bad, ugly Mr. Doubt darkened my doorstep, trying to force his way into our happy homeschool abode, I firmly (though not so politely) shoved him out and slammed the door.

CHAPTER 5:

THIRD CONFESSION

The Sin of Misplaced Trust

"I know God will not give me anything I can't handle. I just wish he didn't trust me so much."
~ Mother Teresa

God has an unusual relationship with us. I mean, here we are in our weak and imperfect human state, barely able to take care of ourselves at times, and who does He place in our trust? Those much weaker and more vulnerable than we are: children. Not only does He entrust them to us, but He expects us to be completely responsible for their physical, spiritual, and emotional growth and development. Wow! I'm with Mother Teresa. I wish he didn't trust me so much.

Nonetheless, this *is* what He expects of us. It comes with the territory.

Lucky for us, there are usually more successes than failures in this parenting game. Unfortunately, in light of those successes, one might be inclined to rely less on God and more on oneself. Though I hate to admit it, as a homeschooling mom, I fell down that rabbit hole for a time, although it wasn't such an unusual result. Once the merry-go-round of homeschooling begins, a newbie inundated with a whole new lifestyle thrust upon her begins to go into survival mode. We ingest, then digest, a smorgasbord of ideas. If we are not careful, the new knowledge and the need to feel competent might make us move into self-reliance, rather that God-reliance.

The Unholy Trinity: Me, Myself, and I

Many people believe a person should always trust her own instincts. After all, you know yourself better than anyone else, so why not have a little more confidence?

Perhaps if we lived in a perfect world, with a perfectly formed conscience, a direct line into the future, and the ability to play out the consequences of any variety of scenarios, we could see the best outcome of any given circumstance and self-trust could work. Find a way to harness such a scenario, and you can sell it, make your millions, and retire in the Bahamas.

It isn't that we cannot trust our assessments. The issue is when left unchecked and underdeveloped, relying too much on oneself can be one of the biggest forms of misplaced trust. Why? That ego-driven perspective is tied very closely to pride, and we all know where pride ultimately leads.

Part of the fallout from being led by our egos is played out in the form of misplaced trust, which completely undermines homeschooling efforts. When our pride-driven ego leads us in the decision-making process, trust may be placed falsely in people or systems that we have inaccurately judged as trustworthy. So, unless failing is part of your homeschool plan, you might want to know where and how to develop authentic trust.

As for me, let's just say it's a good thing I kept a supply of bandages in stock for skinned knees.

Trust in the Vendors and the Convention

Conventions are great! They bring people in a particular industry together for the purpose of encouragement, enlightenment, and education. Homeschool conventions are no different. All things pertinent to my needs are all under one roof. It sounds all too perfect. However, conventions can perpetuate a totally misplaced trust in vendors and/or education systems for several reasons.

Weighing the pros and cons of Math-U-See, versus Abeka, versus Miquon, versus (fill in the bank) can be disastrous for a newcomer, and that's just for math! Consequently, I, like so many other homeschool moms, did the only reasonable thing: I went to a convention!

A convention made perfect sense. As a newbie, I needed guidance. As longtime vendors, they were experts. I felt sure I could trust them to guide me.

My conclusions sounded like good logic, except for one tiny factor: these are businesses, and the purpose of a business is to stay in business. As I looked at them to be my perfect guide, they looked at me to be, bluntly speaking, their paycheck. Although there is nothing wrong with running a business, it would have helped me to analyze the relationship beforehand.

Herein lies the problem in trusting vendors at a convention. Each vendor is completely convincing that their curriculum can solve your problem, fill the hole in your educational abyss, and guarantee your child will be on his way to a 140 IQ and Harvard. Granted, that may be slightly exaggerated, but even so, although they might not use those words, vendors bring an unspoken vague promise of ultimate success through the use of their products.

Another area of enticement is the "convention only" offer, which obviously is only available during the convention. We homeschool families are on very tight budgets, so bargains can easily influence our choices. However, when they are offered under that kind of pressure, they are less of a bargain and more of a sales tactic. We know this from other areas of life, right? Not much different than the unsolicited call, promising an unbeatable deal of "buy now and save." So, how is it that we forget that fact at homeschool conventions? Oh, yeah, it's because this is a *trusted* expert. And he must be offering this great bargain from a completely altruistic perspective.

I am not trying to throw a blanket of suspicion over homeschool conventions, or all vendors and their products. There is much to learn and digest at these One-Stop-Shopping-Extravaganzas. The issue is not the convention or the vendors, but rather our own hearts. If we have not found the true place for our trust, and instead rely on our own perceptions of vendors and their presentations, we can be manipulated into buying products that don't necessarily suit our needs or our child(ren). The Trustworthy One awaits, and He doesn't have a booth under the homeschool convention roof. Conventions are better utilized after first consulting with He Who has your ultimate best interest at heart.

After moving like a deer in the headlights through several homeschool conventions (and making my fair share of poor choices in curriculum purchases), I discovered the importance of knowing who my child is, as God created him. The more I tuned-in to how he learns, the less often I wasted money on curriculum that wasn't geared to his needs. After that, conventions were a joy because my head wasn't turned in a less-than-perfect direction by a well-meaning vendor trying to convince me of the superiority of his company's methodology.

Trusting the Seasoned Ones

We love our friends, don't we? They are there for us in times of great need. New homeschool moms immediately recognize the great need for friends and help at the beginning of this new lifestyle, which is why it's quite natural to turn to those who not only care for us, but have experienced this genesis moment in their own lives. I did likewise.

One of my toughest decisions was in the area of math. First, it was not dearly loved by our son. Second, I was not looking forward to reliving algebra and geometry. I had a long-standing, love-hate relationship with math. So, friend-consulting I went, certain I could trust their judgement.

My first consultant-friend was a Math-U-See advocate. She was homeschooling three children, and all were doing exceptionally well with that program. Her description of the ease of use, along with observing the obvious brilliance of her above-grade-level kids, was convincing. Since my son was a Lego expert, I thought this was a no-brainer. Confidently, I purchased manipulatives and immersed myself in this methodology. In a short time, my confidence waivered, as well as my misplaced trust in this friend's program endorsement. My son was less than interested. When I tried to make a Lego comparison, he looked at me as if I'd just landed in my pod from Mars. Like him, I was having a bit of a disconnect with the whole manipulatives model in general. I envisioned my son in his first year at college pulling out his manipulatives in order to understand calculus. So much for Math-U-See for our family.

My next experience trusting friends' guidance didn't involve a full-blown investment—the Miquon System. Her son also excelled, and our boys were similar in some ways. The great thing here was that my friend graciously loaned us some old books so I could try them out. This system also used manipulatives, I discovered, under the exotic name of Cuisenaire rods. Translation: manipulatives that have a difficult-to-pronounce name and are costly. Since our boy was disinterested in Math-U-See's manipulatives methodology, and Miquon was aimed at primary grades, I immediately dismissed this method.

Jesus, I Trust in You

> *"Let not your hearts be troubled;*
> *believe in God, believe also in me."*
> ~ Jesus Christ, John 14:1

As I begin this section quoting the words of Our Lord, I wonder if anything else can be added. Isn't this the whole idea of our existence? Isn't this the perspective we need in all we do? And why would anyone (i.e., I) ever think anything else? But I will attempt to enlighten what this means to me in the context of homeschooling.

Jesus is the author and perfecter of our faith. The Alpha and Omega, the beginning and end, so isn't it ironic that even in knowing He is completely trustworthy and able, I embarked upon as daunting a task as homeschooling without bringing Him in at the *beginning*? It certainly would have been nice if that voice of Julie Andrews had drifted into my mind with those timeless words of wisdom that might remind me to start at the very beginning.

Somewhere in the trial and error phase, I began to pay attention to the unique individual God created in this precious child entrusted to me, which is where my trust in Jesus was most needed. All the conventions, experts, and friends in the world could not provide for me as God did. My trust in Him brought about much better results.

When I evaluated our boy's way of learning, his logical and systematic way of looking at the world, as well as his newfound love for certain styles of graphics, his needs and learning style became evident. After this analysis and prayer, God led us to the PACE system, which encompassed our son's learning style by offering math in manageable comic-styled booklets that also allowed him to go at his own pace. He developed a new sense of ability and accomplishment. When we saw our son's success in math using the new system, we transitioned to the same format for some of his other subjects.

All of this was only possible after I stopped depending upon people who I initially considered experts, whether professional or acquaintances. Coming to the realization that I was the only expert of my child's strengths and needs, through trusting God's guidance and mercy, was the turning point toward success in our homeschool journey.

Jesus, I trust in you.

Thanks be to God.

CHAPTER 6:

FOURTH CONFESSION

The Sin of Not Understanding Vocation

Marriage is the "foundation for the family, where children learn the values and the virtues that will make good Christians as well as good citizens."
~ United States Conference of Catholic Bishops
Marriage: Love and Life in the Divine Plan

One of the most primal forces in life is the search for significance. Our very souls crave to know that we have mission and purpose in our earthly pilgrimage. However, like many driving forces, the need for significance can be derailed if we are not careful.

In my own journey, I had left the working world in order to be available to raise children, a decision I do not regret. However, there were times I wondered whether my contribution to humanity was fulfilled by taking care of a home filled with children. Throughout my days prior to homeschooling, I began to seek other paths to find the significance that eluded me. Mind you, this was prior to returning to Catholicism, so a term like one's vocation calling was way outside of my frame of reference.

When I first committed to homeschooling our son, my understanding of the task was severely lacking. In my mind, it was like a part-time position, where I might go through the motions of a school day, only to then be freed up for more enjoyable pastimes.

Like all people, I was gifted with my own set of unique talents and skills. Most of these fell into the creative arena. I was a musician, vocalist, songwriter, and crafts person. In my haste to find purpose, I found myself tangent jumping, a fun little game fraught with time-wasting distractions. Interesting, but not targeted like a laser beam on life direction. I tried my hand at many of my skills as I sought significance-affirming pathways. One path was most telling and perhaps a game changer.

In one of my most long-lasting attempts at finding meaning, I sought to develop my music business. Prior to my marriage and my return to Catholicism, I had been a member in various Christian (Protestant) bands and vocal groups. Since that necessitated much time away from home for rehearsals and travel that would have been nearly impossible as a homeschooling mom, I went a different route. Instead, I began to focus on songwriting. Though I believed this would not take up as much time as concerts in the past, I found I was mistaken.

Not only was I anxiously looking for holes in the daily schedule in order to write, it became evident that if I were to succeed in this arena of music, I would need to travel and establish relationships with music professionals in Nashville. I became a Nashville Songwriters Association member, along with other music associations like the Country Music Association. I traveled to Nashville several times, making acquaintances like the secretary at Randy Travis's management office. During this time in my life, I actually had some degree of success. One of my compositions was recorded by a regional Christian group, and one is under contract with a Christian publisher. I was a semi-finalist at Music in the Rockies for a Christian love song, and the same song received semi-finalist ranking in Billboard Magazine's yearly song writing contest. Still another song I wrote after the 9/11 terrorist attacks received a personal letter of thanks from President George H.W. Bush. I also had a song used in a local political campaign.

Somewhere in the midst of my pursuit of songwriting, I came back to the Church. I began to hear about discerning one's vocation. As I said, in my Protestant circles there was no talk of discernment. The whole concept was foreign. I thought it simply meant to seek out your career. Once I discovered the Catholic view of vocation, which has less to do with your skill set and more to do with God's direction for your station in life, my eyes were opened. Looking back on it, the words in Ecclesiastes 1 echo through my mind…

[1]The words of the Preacher, the son of
David, king in Jerusalem.
[2]Vanity of vanities, says the Preacher,
vanity of vanities! All is vanity!
[3]What does man gain by all the toil
at which he toils under the sun?"

And then in Mark 8…

[36]For what does it profit a man, to gain the
whole world and forfeit his life? [37]For what
can a man give in return for his life?

I began to wonder, what exactly was I chasing,
and why?

My father (rest in peace) often used the old adage
"spinning their wheels" when observing someone
pursuing something in futility. That phrase provides
an indisputable mental picture. Was that me? Was
I engaged in a flurry of activity, but going nowhere
fast? If that were true, why?

When I discovered the true meaning of vocation, I had a revelation that made me completely
throw out my previously determined direction. In
the most tangible way, my vocation was already
determined. Whether or not I had done the proper
discernment prior to my Catholicism was moot; I
was married and had a family. In one sense, that was
a comfort. I knew how much my husband and I
loved each other. We were committed to our marriage, and our family was an extension of that love.
That much was out of the way. Whew! But what

did that all mean at this point with respect to my personal significance?

This is where I had to do some real soul-searching. My husband and I knew we had made the best possible decision in homeschooling our son, but it appeared that seeking out significance through creating music was distracting and detracting me from the prime directive. It became pretty clear to me that in order to commit completely to my vocation as a homeschool mom, something had to give.

Re-assess. Re-group. Re-direct.

I'll be the first to admit that making the commitment to mothering and schooling, and abandoning my music wasn't easy. Music has a particular type of allure, and creating music goes a step further. Setting aside that endeavor was not something I would have done before this point in my life, at least not willingly. But, WOW! I immediately made a new discovery by setting music aside—there are actually twenty-four hours in a day, a whole 1,440 minutes! Mind-boggling.

Moving away from seeking significance through music opened up an enormous amount of time. The further away I was from that decision, the more I found my focus where it belonged—on my son's education. I was amazed (and horrified) by how much I merely did the minimum before my re-focus. His education wasn't suffering tremendously before, but was not as good as it could be. That sin was on me.

Even more beneficial was an unexpected benefit that played into discovering my real significance through my homeschooling vocation. Before, I felt accomplishment, an immediate elation, when I finished composing a new song, but that feeling diminished until the time I wrote another one. And then, if my accomplishment was not embraced by the Who's Who in my music world bubble, I felt unfulfilled.

In contrast, once my full attention was on our boy and *his* success and well-being, I understood my true purpose through God's pleasure in a vocational calling done well. Our son's faith and character, along with his developing skills and accomplishments, provided a new sense of significance that I believe was much more pleasing to God. It was much more pleasing to me, too!

What have I gained by my decision to fully embrace my vocation as it applied to our homeschooling journey? Our son is in the early years of young adult life, and at this writing, in his third year of college. He has a good handle on his ethics, morals, and faith. He is intelligent, funny, and great to be around. Of course, much character is his inherent personality, yet I am certain that his forward momentum and development might have been lessened had I continued in my misguided drive to find my own significance outside of my vocation in marriage and family. I would have fallen short, and my purpose not fulfilled to its end.

This is not to say that every mom who home-schools cannot have a vocation to her family, and pursue other things. It gets back to knowing who you are, what is needed to accomplish the task of homeschooling, and what you are capable of handling. Priorities are key. If your Godly vocation becomes hampered by your hobbies, jobs or other interests, it is time to get things in order.

The sin of not fully understanding vocation can complicate homeschooling. It can make us less than enthusiastic as we drudge through the day. It can play out in unnecessary fatigue due to a sense of boredom. In the worst case, incomplete understanding of vocation can be transmitted outwardly in ways that express frustration, dissatisfaction, and perhaps even resentment toward one's family. Truly, no one wants to go there.

I am exceedingly thankful that I finally grasped the meaning of my vocation as a homeschool mom.

CHAPTER 7:

PENANCE AND ABSOLUTION

Okay, I blew it. Now what?

"Where sin was hatched,
let tears now wash the nest."
~ Saint Robert Southwell

Parents are no strangers to tears; this is a fact of life. Yet as common as tears are to parents, are we aware that they bring healing in times of stress? In his article, "The Miracle of Tears," Jerry Bergman says, "Tears are just one of many miracles which work so well that we take them for granted every day."[1]

According to *Psychology Today*, "Biochemist and 'tear expert' Dr. William Frey at the Ramsey Medical Center in Minneapolis discovered that reflex tears are 98% water, whereas emotional tears also contain stress hormones which get excreted from the body

---

[1] Jerry, Bergman, "The Miracle of Tears," *Creation* 15, no. 4 (September 1993): 16:18.

through crying."[2] Endorphins are released, which reduce pain and improve mood. Toxins are carried from the body through tears. So, imagine just how necessary is the cleansing and healing property of tears to homeschool moms!

Saint Robert Southwell's insight gives another perspective to the tears we homeschool moms shed after we've realized the effects of sins and missteps in our methodology. As Saint Southwell so aptly describes, the nest is "washed." What a great visual!

Think about those times when you've just completed a spring-cleaning frenzy. I'm not talking about the quick, wipe-across-the-counters-to-find-a-space-to-prepare-sandwiches kind of clean. I'm talking deep, scrape-off-the-grime kind of clean. You know the kind. The kind where dirt and clutter that may have been there since…well…last spring are whisked away. That's the kind of nest-cleaning to which Saint Southwell alludes. It has purpose. It gives a fresh start.

Moms, hear this loud and clear: your tears are not a sign weakness or failure. In fact, they are more often a sign of clarity and knowledge gained. They signify that, although you may have committed a sin, you are aware, repentant, and readied for penance so that you may receive absolution in order to

---

[2] Judith Orloff, M.D, "The Health Benefits of Tears," *Psychology Today*, July 27, 2010, accessed December 30, 2018, https://www.psychologytoday.com/us/blog/emotional-freedom/201007/the-health-benefits-tears.

go and sin no more…or at least less. So, allow yourself to lament, even to cry. You will be better for it on the other side.

Penance Through Prayer

Penance provides for the penitent specific actions after confession in order to become more like Jesus. What a perfect goal for homeschool moms! If we can learn to think and respond like Jesus, then homeschool decisions will never fail. But, whoa! Remember, this is a process. Be joyful for the journey, and know that although perfection is the goal, small victories can and should be celebrated. Let's take a look at how to live in a state of penance in our role as homeschoolers.

A life of penance is one of conversion. But to what are we converting as homeschool moms? We know we have come *from* blunders which undermined our forward momentum. What we hope for is that our conversion from homeschool sins will project us *to* right decisions.

When we review and confess the sins of the past, we see that they many times have lacked an important component: prayer. Oh, sure. The prayers are loud and strong after the fact, while we try to pick up the pieces and salvage any possible good from our mistakes. But the prayers of preparation, rather than reparation, were what we needed at the onset. Part of living a life of penance means to commit to prayer on the front end of decisions or changes to any current direction.

Penance through Conforming to Christ's Example

A life of penance is a continual striving to convert from the human way of doing things to God's way. According to Christ, our goal is to live with the needs of others placed above our own needs. In loving the Lord our God with all our hearts, minds, souls and strength, we are well on the road to penitential living. Most Catholic homeschool moms I know love God with their whole lives. But there's another part to that passage in Matthew: Love thy neighbor as thyself.

Here is where too many homeschool moms fall short, myself included. Selfless living is what we do best. It's a huge part of that vocation thing. We are the nurturers, the caregivers, the chauffeurs, the personal shoppers and wear countless other hats in or vocational role as wives and moms. By most standards, we Catholic homeschool moms appear to be living out our vocations well. But are we? Aren't we forgetting the model for all Catholics?

Jesus was the model of how to live vocation as He served humanity. He spent his days teaching and healing *ad infinitum*. But even Jesus knew when it was time to recharge His battery. Mark 4:35-36 records that Jesus found it necessary to leave the crowds by taking a boat to the other side of the water; we are even told in verse 38 that Jesus was asleep at the stern of the boat, a method for recharging the body and mind. It apparently was a regular practice for Jesus to move away from His vocational activities for the purpose of refreshment. In Luke 5:16 we find that although His ministry was to be among and serve people, Jesus would often retreat to deserted places to pray. Similarly, in Mark 6:30-32, we see that He withdrew for the purpose of rest. Through His example, we see that occasional retreating from vocational demands is necessary in order to live our vocations well.

How are you doing on "me time"? In order to be the best Catholic homeschool mom you can be, to make the best possible God-directed homeschool decisions, and to avoid so much stress build-up that those nest-cleansing tears are a daily (or hourly) occurrence, you need a break!

There are many moms who do not understand the meaning of downtime. They say they are taking a break, but once on said break they use that time to read up on homeschool methods or ideas. People, think about it. How can you be on a break when your break becomes a mini-seminar on the very thing from which you are supposed to be breaking? Instead, find things that truly will refresh your spirit. Find a hobby. Learn a new language. Take walks. Read a book (teacher's manuals don't count.) Whatever you choose, just be sure it is an actual break from all you do as a homeschooler. This is how you can truly love yourself. Subsequently, how you care for yourself will be reflected in how you treat your neighbor, and your nearest neighbors are the members of your family and homeschool.

Penance through Complete Openness to God

According to Monsignor Jeffrey A. Ingham, "While penance is part of reparation for sin, it is above all an emptying of self to allow for an openness to God."[3] The best ways for this to happen is to be in His presence at Mass and Adoration, to steep yourself in prayer, and to frequent the Sacraments. As we utilize all the graces God has for us, our hearts become more open to all God desires for us, including penance. The USCCB website describes the penitential life like this:

> One important way to grow in the Lord is to observe the penitential practices that strengthen us for resisting temptation, allow us to express our sorrow for the sins we have committed, and help to repair the tear caused by our sinning...Penitential practices take many forms: apologizing to an injured party, healing divisions within our families, fasting during the Lenten season, or graciously accepting the menial tasks of

[3] Monsignor Jeffrey A. Ingham, "Renewal and the Penitential Life," *Homiletic & Pastoral Review*, October 2, 2018, accessed January 2, 2019, https://www.hprweb.com/2018/10/renewal-and-the-penitential-life/.

life. The purpose of penance is not to diminish life but to enrich it.[4]

Not to diminish life, but enrich it. Who doesn't want that? Two areas in the above paragraph are worth discussion: apologizing to an injured party, and graciously accepting the menial tasks of life.

Okay, Say You're Sorry

Looking back at a few of the homeschool sins I committed, it wasn't just myself who suffered. None of us live in a vacuum. We live in community within our own homes, and there are others who either benefit or suffer along with us. As I fumbled along through some of my homeschool messes, my boy suffered through the blunder as much as I did. My frustration was centrally focused, primarily because each mistake caused me to reassess, spend more money, then go once again through the curriculum learning curve I'd come to despise. *My* time was wasted. *My* money flew out the door. It affected me, me…and, oh yeah, me!

But as my frustration played out, many times I was forced to admit that in my haste to jump on a particular curriculum bandwagon, I rode right past (sometimes over) my son. Then, when frustration

---

[4] "Penitential Practices for Today's Catholics," United States Conference of Catholic Bishops, accessed January 2, 2019, http://www.usccb.org/prayer-and-worship/liturgical-year/lent/penitential-practices-for-todays-catholics.cfm.

levels were high, certain virtues took a hiatus, likely too embarrassed by my behavior to stick around. After those times of impatience, the ability to apologize to my son was a healing balm.

Time for a reality check. Knowing we have wronged another is one thing, but being able to own up to it and to ask forgiveness is a whole other ballgame. The only way to find the ability to survive this kind of honesty with one's child is to be a child who is honest with God. Our first apology should be to Him. After all, we likely left Him out of the equation. But more importantly, staying close to Him in the Sacraments and through prayer makes a difficult penance, such as apologizing to your child, possible. Then it's tears, hugs, and kisses. Then, VOILA! Forgiveness from your own child in this penance helps to heal your soul. Who knew?

Finding Meaning in the Mundane

"Oh, joy! Here's another week of lessons to plan;
be still, my heart."

How can taking on menial tasks with joy help me fine-tune my rough edges and atone for my homeschool goofs? For help with this one, I went to my favorite gameshow: ASK AN APOSTLE!

First, I found this tidbit from James, the Apostle: "Count it all joy, my brethren, when you meet various trials, for you know that the testing of your faith produces steadfastness" (James 1:2-3).

If we take this verse seriously, trials, even menial ones, offer opportunity for our faith to persevere. Now, there's a handy little trait to acquire. Knowing perseverance will be the byproduct of taking on a menial task, we can approach it more graciously and accept this form of penance.

However, I found this instruction from Saint Paul to be a game changer: "Whatever your task, work heartily, as if serving the Lord and not men" (Colossians 3:23).

Did he just say, "Whatever your task"? Yes, even what might appear to be the drudgery of lesson planning is to be done for the Lord. Yet even more interesting are the verses before and after. In the preceding verse, slaves are being told to obey their human masters with simplicity of heart. However, the verse which follows completes the thought. We aren't slaves to the drudgery or to the tasks at hand. We are to be slaves only to the Lord, Jesus Christ. He is the Good Task Master, who offers inheritance as our reward. Now, that is the perspective I needed in order to live out this penance well.

Absolution: Am I Forgiven, Truly Forgiven?

You have probably heard that God is the God of second chances. And third. And fourth. Thanks be to God!

How many times and in how many ways can a human being mess up? We are told when asked how often to forgive another that the number is uncountable: seventy times seven. (Math nerds need not calculate that for me.) The phrase is meant to be a symbol of forgiveness. We are to forgive others in the same way, and in the same frequency that God forgives the penitent heart.

Which brings us back to the whole idea of this book on my own confessions as a homeschool mom. When we confess, and sometimes the same sin comes up, the priest is compassionate. He offers the help we need to work harder toward overcoming even recurrent sins. That is the heart of God, played out in the priest, *in persona Christi capitis*: in the person of Christ the head. We can be just as confident in complete forgiveness for our foolish errors as Catholic homeschool moms. God is good. God forgives.

We are all prodigal sons and daughters. We have the promise of all we need by the hand of God, yet we turn and go our own ways, even in our homeschooling. But guess what? God is still there through our trials. He watches and waits. As he sees our newly embraced penitent life of conversion, forgiveness abounds and His grace is poured out, grace that gives us the ability to go and avoid the near occasions of sin in the future. The penance we live and God's forgiveness for our homeschool sins help shape us into even better, stronger, homeschool moms, which is the ultimate benefit of living a joyful, penitent lifestyle.

CONCLUSION

What does It all mean?

"Children are our most valuable resource."
~Herbert Hoover,
31st President of the United States

President Hoover's observation about children has been reiterated many times. Likely, one of the most common rephrasing is that children are the future. Well, of course they are. In most cases, they will grow to adulthood, while their parents and grandparents pass on. How, then, does homeschooling effectively grow our children into the valuable resources President Hoover saw?

One way is that by homeschooling we learn to appreciate more fully the value of each child within the family. Because homeschooled children are present all day, rather than away for six hours a day, each child's unique qualities can be nurtured. Their individual contribution to the home, whether it is household chores or something as simple as reading to a younger sibling, becomes a vital part in how the home functions. Each homeschool is a micro-society that is similar in design to the greater society at large. The goal is to develop members who contribute well. Consequently, the homeschooling family has a much greater impact toward that end merely by having their children under their direct care throughout the entire day, fine-tuning and developing each child's role.

Another way that President Hoover's observation is realized in a homeschool setting is in the development of character, ethics, and virtue. Even the parents of publicly educated children desire their children to become ethical members of society. Unfortunately, as discussed earlier, those in the public setting during the formative years are exposed to poor peer examples which, sadly, some emulate. The end result in many cases is a child who was raised well at home, but fell prey to a desire to fit in with friends, which then played out in him following the pack. Even the best parents have experienced this sad phenomenon. Conversely, when children remain in the home environment, with parents carefully designing socialization opportunities that won't compromise family values, the children are not exposed to contradictory behaviors that might lure them into a negative change of their own behavior. In essence, the homeschool method of socialization is of great benefit to society.

Finally, President Hoover would likely appreciate that homeschool families generally develop future members of society who can process information logically and think for themselves. Much of our society has been agenda-driven in recent years, and those agendas run rampant within the walls of public education. What used to take up the school day in the three Rs has been replaced by a social experiment that molds minds into acceptance of the current politically correct trends.

Don't get me wrong. Extreme bullying should be discouraged, and acceptance of people who are not like ourselves is commendable. Caring for the environment is a fine goal. Unfortunately, rather than be accepting, as they claim they are, schools approach these social issues in ways that marginalize anyone who has a different approach or belief. Teachers promote politics and politicians openly in lectures, and the pressure to think like the masses is a constant companion during school years from as early as kindergarten. The real advantage to homeschooling is the nurturing of the family's worldview, faith, and values. Equally noteworthy is that the political whims of administrators and educators do not replace or take time away from the purpose of school: education. And in this setting, open discussion can allow the student to process and develop logic and opinion without the pressure to conform to an agenda-driven education system.

In spite of all the benefits, homeschooling is not a quick and easy decision. There are many parents who hesitate as I did at the daunting idea of educating their children at home. Such an enormous step can be frightening, but nearly all students can benefit from homeschooling. Aside from the educational benefits in home education, there are social perks. Children in the home education model are offered more guidance in peer groups and deal with a minimum of bullying that might otherwise chip away at their confidence. Because of the more intimate setting, parent educators can quickly spot areas of educational issues that need to be addressed. Consequently, students are able to move more at their own pace, ensuring actual learning rather than simply being pushed along through each grade level. In contrast to the benefits of home education, a great many students struggle in public schools. Even worse, some continue in that struggle post-graduation as they try to find their way as young adults, which is tragic for the individual and society. Homeschooling can and does minimize the struggle to learn and apply studies to life.

In some ways, your homeschool journey may resemble mine. Perhaps like me you had a one-toe-at-a-time experience, until you were totally submerged. Or maybe you dove in headfirst. Or perhaps you're standing on the shore, admiring the other swimmers but unsure of your swimming stamina. Regardless of where you are, this is your journey. It is unique to you and your family. Whether you believe it or not, you can do this!

Beware of the pitfalls. Many of the sins previously outlined can be avoided if you embark on the journey with sufficient spiritual preparation.

First, the sin of letting temptation rule your decisions can undermine success. When God allows temptation in our lives, it is to lead us toward greater faith by rejecting that which will draw us away from Him. In our homeschooling decisions, we must reject the temptation of imitating the model of public schools or succumbing to envy of how others might homeschool. Remember that temptation can be a tool toward sanctification provided we avoid yielding to its allure.

The sin of doubt can also be a huge hurdle. It is not that doubt will never rear its ugly head. Know in advance that doubts will arise. However, if you have prepared, the Lord can help you dismiss unjustified doubt, replacing it with a healthier perspective based on his promise that He will be with you in all you do. Doubt, if approached well, can launch us toward greater trust in God.

Which leads to the sin of misplaced trust. This sin insidiously creeps in, once we surrender to the sin of doubt. Through unchecked doubt, we can be led to believe that others and their perspectives are worthy of our trust. If we rely on the perceived expertise of others without balancing it with our complete trust in God, we can easily miss God's direction for our homeschooling choices. To avoid falling into this sin, you need to first be immersed in prayer before seeking out and listening to others. Pray for direction. Pray for God to illuminate what is needed. Then pray for Him to bring the right people along to guide you into the best decisions.

Ultimately, it is only God in whom we place our complete trust.

Finally, though a natural God-given desire, the desire for significance may morph into misunderstanding your calling. This sin denies who you are to God. The key to avoiding this pitfall is in understanding the great privilege we have in the vocation of our marriage and family. Raising children and homeschooling them is a tremendous good work in the Kingdom! If you are chosen for this vocation, God is working in and through you so that you can present your homeschooled child to the world and to God to be a blessing for the good of society and God's people. Remember God's mandate in Proverbs 22:6; the loving training of your child now will stay with him in his future. Don't underestimate the importance of your vocation. God certainly does not.

Confession is very good for the soul, offering us the opportunity to purge, repent, and receive forgiveness. More importantly, confession helps us to move on and away from sin. I thank God for his patience with me even during my errors in homeschooling.

May God bless you and guide you and your family as you travel the road to your homeschooling success! *Ad majorem Dei gloriam*—For the greater Glory of God!

~ Finis

BIBLIOGRAPHY

Bergman, Jerry. "The Miracle of Tears." *Creation* 15, no. 4 (September 1993): 16:18.

Ingham, Monsignor Jeffrey A. "Renewal and the Penitential Life." *Homiletic & Pastoral Review.* October 2, 2018. Accessed January 2, 2019. https://www.hprweb.com/2018/10/renewal-and-the-penitential-life/.

Marriage: Love and Life in the Divine Plan, A Pastoral Letter of the United States Conference of Catholic Bishops. United States Conference of Catholic Bishops, 2009.

Orloff, Judith, M.D. "The Health Benefits of Tears." *Psychology Today.* July 27, 2010. Accessed December 30, 2018. https://www.psychologytoday.com/us/blog/emotional-freedom/201007/the-health-benefits-tears.

Penitential Practices for Today's Catholics. United States Conference of Catholic Bishops. Accessed January 2, 2019. http://www.usccb.org/prayer-and-worship/liturgical-year/lent/penitential-practices-for-todays-catholics.cfm.

SELECT RESOURCES LIST

Homeschool Connections
Online Catholic courses for high school, middle school, and grade school. Offers high school dual enrollment with Franciscan University.
888-372-4757
https://homeschoolconnectionsonline.com/

Home School Legal Defense Association (HSLDA)
A must if you private homeschool.
540-388-5600
https://hslda.org/

Kolbe Academy
Catholic, Ignatian, classical education. Offers traditional homeschooling, online courses, and self-paced courses.
707-255-6499
https://kolbe.org/

Little Saints—A Catholic Preschool Program
Imprimatur by Bishop Fabian Bruskewitz, host of EWTN's "In Persona Christi."
www.catholicpreschool.com

Mother of Divine Grace School
Accredited by the Western Association of Schools and Colleges (ACS WASC). A Catholic distance education program based on Laura Berquist's *Designing your Own Classical Curriculum*.
805-646-5818
https://modg.org/

Our Lady of Victory School
Accredited by the National Association of Private Catholic & Independent Schools (NAPCIS). Home study program.
208-773-7265
https://www.olvs.org/

Seton Homeschooling
Under the bishop of Arlington, VA. Catholic homeschooling for pre-K to 12. Also offers special education services for children with learning or medical challenges. Accredited by AdvancED.
866-280-1930
https://www.setonhome.org

T.O.R.C.H. (Traditions of Roman Catholic Homes)
Network of Catholic support groups throughout the United States.

About Leonine Publishers

Leonine Publishers LLC makes fine Catholic literature available to Catholics throughout the English-speaking world. Leonine Publishers offers an innovative "hybrid" approach to book publication that helps authors as well as readers. Please visit our web site at www.leoninepublishers.com to learn more about us. Browse our online bookstore to find more solid Catholic titles to uplift, challenge, and inspire.

Our patron and namesake is Pope Leo XIII, a prudent, yet uncompromising pope during the stormy years at the close of the 19th century. Please join us as we ask his intercession for our family of readers and authors.

www.leoninepublishers.com

www.ingramcontent.com/pod-product-compliance
Lightning Source LLC
Chambersburg PA
CBHW030106070426
42448CB00037B/1115